# GECKOS

by Imogen Kingsley

AMICUS | AMICUS INK

Amicus High Interest and Amicus Ink are published by Amicus
P.O. Box 1329, Mankato, MN 56002
www.amicuspublishing.us

Library of Congress Cataloging-in-Publication Data
Names: Kingsley, Imogen, author.
Title: Geckos / by Imogen Kingsley.
Description: Mankato, Minnesota : Amicus/Amicus Ink, [2019] | Series:
  Lizards in the wild | Audience: K to Grade 3. | Includes index.
Identifiers: LCCN 2018004180 (print) | LCCN 2018006677 (ebook) | ISBN
  9781681515946 (pdf) | ISBN 9781681515564 (library binding) | ISBN
  9781681523941 (paperback)
Subjects:  LCSH: Geckos--Juvenile literature.
Classification: LCC QL666.L245 (ebook) | LCC QL666.L245 K56 2019 (print) |
  DDC 597.95/2--dc23
LC record available at https://lccn.loc.gov/2018004180

Photo Credits: Shutterstock/Dobermaraner, cover, PhotoSt, 2, 22,
WORAKON PHUAPHAN, 5, Shane Myers Photography, 6, Anna Veselova, 9,
Wasu Watcharadachaphong, 13, Cathy Keifer, 14, yingtustocker, 17; Alamy/
blickwinkel/Teigler, 10–11; iStock/Dkart, 18, CMP1975, 21

Editor: Mary Ellen Klukow
Designer: Peggie Carley
Photo Researcher: Holly Young

Printed in China

HC 10 9 8 7 6 5 4 3 2 1
PB 10 9 8 7 6 5 4 3 2 1

# TABLE OF CONTENTS

# A LOUD LIZARD

A gecko is loud. It clicks. It barks. It hisses. It even makes a gecko-gecko sound. No other lizards can make these sounds.

5

# WHERE THEY LIVE

Geckos live in warm places all over the world. They are **cold-blooded**. They need the sun to keep warm. Antarctica is the only continent where they do not live.

## Check This Out

Australia is home to 60 kinds of geckos.

# MANY COLORS

There are more than 1,600 kinds of geckos. They come in many colors. A gecko is often the same color as its **habitat**. This makes it hard for **predators** to see it.

9

# HABITAT

Geckos are found in many habitats. Banded geckos live in the desert. Long-toed Geckos live in the forest. Some geckos live in the mountains.

# BIG AND LITTLE

The Tokay gecko is big. It can be over 1 foot (30 cm) long. The smallest gecko is the Jaragua lizard. It can fit on a dime!

# A NIGHT HUNTER

Most geckos are **nocturnal**. They hunt at night. They eat bugs. They eat fruit. They sometimes eat other geckos.

# COOL EYES

A gecko has big eyes. It has thin **pupils**. It has clear eyelids that protect its eyes. A gecko sees in color. It even sees color in the dark!

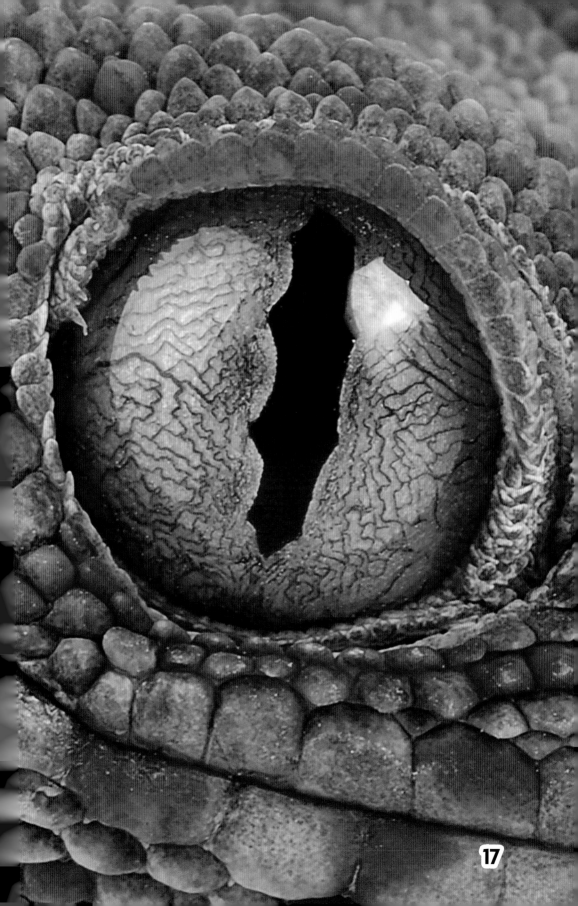

# TAILS AND TOES

A gecko has pads on its toes. The pads have sticky hairs. They help the gecko climb. It climbs to hide from predators.

## Check This Out
Predators can bite off a gecko's tail. But it can grow back!

# YOUNG GECKOS

A mother gecko lays eggs in a safe spot. A gecko hatches from an egg. It has an **egg tooth** to break its shell. The baby gecko can take care of itself. It can run and hunt.

# A LOOK AT A GECKO

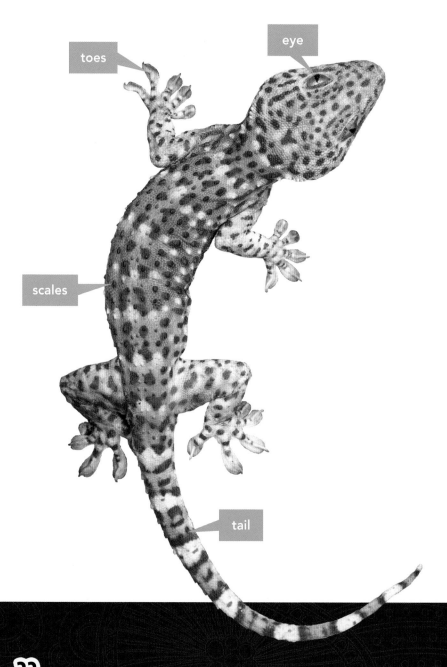

toes

eye

scales

tail

# WORDS TO KNOW

**cold-blooded** Having a body temperature that is similar to its surroundings.

**egg tooth** A small sharp tooth that helps a lizard break out of its shell.

**habitat** The place an animal lives.

**nocturnal** Active at night.

**predator** An animal that hunts other animals for food.

**pupil** The black part of the eye that lets in light.

# LEARN MORE

**Books**

Brett, Flora. *Get to Know Geckos*. North Mankato, Minn.: Capstone Press, 2015.

Macheske, Felicia. *Smiling and Spotted*. Ann Arbor, Mich.: Cherry Lake Publishing, 2017.

Rudolph, Jessica. *Gecko*. New York: Bearport Publishing, 2016.

**Websites**

**DK Find Out!: Lizards**
https://www.dkfindout.com/us/animals-and-nature/reptiles/lizards/

**National Geographic Kids: The Gecko**
https://kids.nationalgeographic.com/animals/gecko

**San Diego Zoo: Lizards**
http://animals.sandiegozoo.org/animals/lizard

# INDEX